WHAT ROMAN CATHOLICS NEED TO KNOW ABOUT PROTESTANTS

ROBERT R. LAROCHELLE

Energion Publications
Gonzalez, FL
2014

Copyright © 2014, Robert R. LaRochrlle

ISBN10: 1-63199-006-3
ISBN13: 978-1-63199-006-9

Energion Publications
P.O. Box 841
Gonzalez, FL 32560

energionpubs.com
pubs@energion.com

WHY THIS BOOK?

Over the last several years, events on the world stage have led to an increased need for interreligious understanding. Most prominently, the aftermath of September 11, 2001 precipitated a necessary rise in interest concerning the Islamic faith. Deeper understanding of different religious perspectives is a necessary antidote against the unfortunate increase in prejudice and mistrust of the unknown. These responses are quite often born out of a lack of knowledge and unnecessary fear.

From time to time, news reports lead people to want to know more about particular religious cults (classic examples include the mass suicide in Jonestown, Guyana and the killings in Waco, Texas). At other times, people are drawn to stories which illuminate for them aspects of long standing religions such as Judaism or Christianity, especially as they interact with friends and co-workers who are part of traditions other than their own. Immigration patterns in different geographic locations have led to a need for increased knowledge of religious traditions from the East, in particular Hinduism and Buddhism.

As I see it, religious literacy is an important component in human understanding and must never be underestimated or underappreciated. It is within the context of this position of mine that I wish to revisit the understanding Roman Catholics have of Protestant faith. Within the United States, of course, most of those who have expressed a religious preference have traditionally identified themselves as Protestants or Catholics. This remains such, even though studies have shown that the numbers are definitely changing! While those looking at these two Christian traditions from the outside might rightfully note striking similarities, there remains to this day significant **differences** between them. These differences need to be explored more fully so their similarities might best be understood.

1

THE IMPORTANCE OF THIS DISCUSSION

In a companion volume to this book entitled *What Protestants Need to Know About Roman Catholics*, I stated several reasons why an examination of this topic is important. In addition to its significance for those who simply wish to understand more about organized religion and its various movements, this subject has meaning on an interpersonal level as well!

Many Catholics, as example, have good friends, partners, significant others, or spouses who happen to be Protestant. In family situations, couples need to make decisions regarding the religious upbringing of their children. In local communities, neighbors live side by side and participate in similar civic activities, yet worship at different churches, oftentimes only visiting other houses of worship for the occasion of a wedding, funeral or some other important public rite. **As I see it, they often exist in parallel religious universes with limited awareness of the common bonds they share.**

One brief note before I continue: Throughout this volume, I will use the terms Catholic Church and Roman Catholic Church interchangeably. All Christians who profess the Nicene or Apostles Creed recognize in it the phrase 'one, holy, catholic and apostolic church.' The context of its usage there is the definition of catholic as universal. Thus, it is quite legitimate to say that the Protestant shares with all other Christians a common faith in Jesus as Lord and Savior. In other words, all Protestants are really 'catholic' with a lower case 'c'.

The terms Catholic Church and Roman Catholic Church refer to the institution in which the Pope is acknowledged as the leader. Catholics tend to prefer the term 'Catholic' when referring to their institutional church. Many Protestants like to make the distinction of Roman Catholic. As I see merits in both terms, I tend to use them interchangeably and will do so in this work.

In this short volume, I am hoping to help those who are Roman Catholic understand the Protestant tradition better. I would really like to see this volume, as well as its companion work to which I have alluded, be a resource for discussion in homes and in churches. I encourage you to use it as a resource for interpersonal discussion and possible study in Adult Education classes and youth ministry settings. In addition, I wish to suggest that campus ministers and teachers in high schools that are religiously affiliated, consider using these little books as starting points for exploration and discussion.

In my view, a healthy recognition of differences need not be an impediment to Christian **unity**. Above all, I have written these works in order to promote the efforts of an **ecumenical** approach to Christian faith. In other words, I contend Catholics and Protestants alike, despite differences that have accrued over the centuries, share with one another a solid **core** of Christian faith that needs to be both recognized and celebrated. While there are those within both traditions less enthusiastic than I about finding and affirming this ecumenical center, it seems clear to me the task of doing so is one of the most important responsibilities of leaders and educators within the Christian churches today.

The alternatives to this effort would seem to be either a willingness to retreat into old stereotypes of what constitutes Protestantism or Catholicism or to make peace with a sense of indifferentism by which the issues themselves are rendered unimportant. Both approaches are dangerous! As I see it, neither of these alternatives is palatable in consideration of the prayer of Jesus, as recorded in the seventeenth chapter of John's Gospel. In this passage, Jesus is presented as praying that those who seek to be His disciples might '*all* **be one**' (John 17:21).

The task, as I see it therefore, is to celebrate a **oneness** that exists even as there are differences. A oneness, in fact, might even be able to develop more fully as those who seek it learn from those differences and integrate what they have learned into both their worship and their activity as they strive to follow Jesus! In other words, I think it would be wonderful were Protestants to be willing to incorporate into their expressions of faith some traditionally

3

'Catholic' practices and vice versa. This can and must be accomplished **without** sacrificing **core** theological principles.

MY BACKGROUND

While I most certainly have an academic interest in this topic, I would be less than honest with you if I did not acknowledge my own autobiographical background. I explored this in detail in the lengthier volume I have written entitled *Crossing the Street* (Energion, 2012). Much of what I say in this short book is explained in considerable depth in that work.

At the time of this writing, I am sixty one years old. I am serving in my fourteenth year as a pastor in a Protestant denomination, the United Church of Christ. For the first forty five years of my life, I was a Roman Catholic. I went to Catholic elementary school, prep school, college and graduate school. I was taught by the Daughters of the Holy Spirit, the Marian Fathers and the Jesuits and I came close to entering the seminary and becoming a Paulist priest! I served as an altar boy at the national headquarters of a group of Catholic sisters for ten years, ultimately achieving the status of head altar boy! My wife of thirty three years and my three children are Roman Catholics. One, my daughter, currently serves as a Catholic campus minister at a college in New York State and will soon be pursuing a Ph.D. in theology from a Jesuit run Catholic university.

For close to twenty years, I worked professionally within the Roman Catholic Church. Over that period of time, I was a religion teacher in Catholic high schools, a Religious Education Director in several parishes, a youth minister on the parish level and a member of a Diocesan staff. In addition, while never ordained a Catholic priest, I was ordained to the Permanent Diaconate in the Catholic Church. In that capacity, I preached on a regular basis, led a variety of church services, baptized over two hundred individuals, conducted a large number of weddings and funerals, assisted people in obtaining annulments and coordinated educational programs designed to help people enter the Catholic Church from other religious traditions or none at all. I have had much experience leading traditional Catholic devotions and rituals, e.g. Stations of the Cross, Benediction of the Blessed Sacrament and wake services. I was even a member of the Knights of Columbus, a well known Catholic men's organization, for several years as well.

My Transition and My Current Situation

At the age of forty five, I both left the Catholic Church and decided to pursue ordained ministry in a Protestant church community. The decision to leave, detailed in *Crossing the Street*, was a difficult one. Unlike what one often hears about people leaving Catholicism, I left with the deepest regard and gratitude for the education I received as a Catholic and for the spiritual experiences that shaped my life. I am, in no way, shape or form, an angry ex-Catholic.

As a new member of different Protestant congregations and ultimately as an ordained clergyperson in two, I have had interesting experiences, both in coming to a deeper understanding of Protestant Christianity, and in serving congregations in which there are a number of former Catholics. At this point historically, for a variety of reasons, many local Protestant congregations in the United States are comprised of former Catholics.

While I could write at great length about the various ways in which my own spirituality has been influenced by both Catholic and Protestant traditions, **my intention in this little book is to help Roman Catholics come to a better understanding of Protestant faith**. In doing so, I am both writing as one raised Catholic who has had the opportunity to do that **and** without any intention of trying to persuade those who are Catholic to make the same decision I did. I simply cannot say that more forcefully or say it enough. In my honest view, religious decisions are complicated ones and the most important task for anyone who claims to follow Jesus is to be the very best disciple she or he can be, living out that discipleship in the church community that makes the most sense for that person.

I write this all realizing that the choice of that community is not always clear cut. Instead it is influenced by a variety of factors: familial, intellectual, and cultural, to cite but a few. With this being said, I am hopeful that this brief work might help in the simple task of helping us all in finding common ground as followers of Jesus.

THE DIFFERENT VARIETIES OF PROTESTANTISM

Anyone reading this book who is a Roman Catholic or was raised as one knows that when you are talking about the Catholic Church to a Protestant, you can describe it simply as a church whose central headquarters is in Rome and under the leadership of someone who holds the office of Pope. Please note: Catholicism is not quite that simply explained as I point out at length in my other writings **but** this little description does point the hearer in the right direction. Incomplete as it may be, the answer gets at the importance of **visible unity** in Catholicism's understanding of itself.

It is far more difficult to explain Protestantism that simply to the Catholic hearer or reader. As an example, within just a few miles of where my church is located in Connecticut, you will find all kinds of different churches, all of which would qualify under the umbrella term 'Protestant.' You will have churches who call themselves Congregational and also UCC, others that are Congregational but certainly aren't United Church of Christ, Lutherans of both an ELCA and Missouri Synod, churches within Anglican Christianity such as the Protestant Episcopal Church of America and still other Anglicans who broke away from those Episcopalians, Presbyterians who are part of the PCUSA and other Presbyterians who split from them ... and I am just beginning to warm up here!!

In fact, if you look at other parts of the country, you will find Protestant churches that are nowhere to be found here in my native New England, the Disciples of Christ as but one example!

My point here is that if you are a Roman Catholic and trying to understand Protestantism, this can get mighty confusing! Unlike the Catholic Church, you can't just point to a Pope in Rome. It's a lot more complicated!

Two Important Points

Now, before we go on any further, however, it is important that we make two very important points:

» Understanding Catholicism is really not as simple as I have described it above. If you were raised Catholic and know many other Catholics, you have probably noticed that not all Catholics act alike, think alike or even pray alike. Depending on your local parish, you may have learned certain prayers and devotions while friends of yours in other Catholic churches have no connection with them. Some Catholics emphasize the veneration of certain saints (example: the Irish and Patrick); others, different saints or they have little focus on saints at all. Catholics reading this who attended colleges taught by, for example, the Dominicans or the Jesuits, are usually somewhat skilled in citing some differences between those two religious orders of priests. There are differences in style and points of emphasis and influences in their respective theologies.

You are indeed probably quite cognizant of the reality that not all Catholics think alike, even when church teaching is pretty firm on certain issues. You know that in spite of the church's official insistence that abortion, artificial birth control and homosexual acts are objectively wrong, there are an awful lot of church going Catholics who see those issues differently from what is taught by 'the church.' You are also probably quite aware that there is a great difference of opinion in the church regarding where dissenting Catholics actually fit into the big picture of the church!

» Understanding Protestantism, while complicated, is far from impossible. While Protestantism, by its very nature, has led to a splitting off process whereby new churches crop up because of dissension within an older church, there really is a **core** of significant Protestant beliefs and tendencies.

As we explore current groupings of Protestant churches, please keep these facts in mind. After we have delved into our exploration of these groups in some detail, we will come back and take a look at some general Protestant tendencies.

GROUPINGS OF PROTESTANTS

Understanding Protestantism is easier if we veer away from distinguishing, say, Lutheranism from Presbyterianism or similar enterprises and look at groupings within the Protestant community which cut across denominations and which explain the ease of the Protestant phenomenon of denominational switching over the course of a lifetime. With this in mind, I suggest that we identify these as significant historic groupings of Protestant churches: *mainline, evangelical/conservative, fundamentalist, Pentecostal, emergent.*

Mainline churches: These are generally in direct line with the churches which sprung out of the historic Reformation of the sixteenth century in Europe, the movement which, simply put, moved Christianity away from its primary one church dominance within Europe and into its current status. In the United States, a nation established by Europeans, these have been the dominant Protestant churches in terms of prominence and cultural influence for much of this country's history. These Protestant churches have experienced the greatest numerical and financial decline since the 1960's. These include (not limited to) the Episcopal Church, the United Methodist Church, the Presbyterian Church USA, the United Church of Christ, the Reformed Church in America, the Disciples of Christ, the American Baptist churches and the Evangelical Lutheran Church in America.

Evangelical/conservative churches: Generally, these church communities have viewed mainline churches as pushing a 'liberal' social and theological agenda which has strayed from what they see

8

as essential Biblical Christianity. Evangelical conservatives generally feel mainline churches have abandoned an emphasis on personal salvation and important teachings central to the Bible in favor of a more 'social Gospel' approach. In fairness, there has been movement in these churches toward a stronger social justice orientation and an embrace of 'social liberal' causes in recent years.

These churches tend to be troubled by the way many mainline churches have embraced same sex marriage and homosexuals in the clergy. It should be noted that more conservative Christians are present in the mainline denominations and, in many cases, have formed organized groups within them. However, over the last two decades, they have found it increasingly difficult to exist within mainline churches. In my own denomination, this has led to a good number of local congregations shedding the UCC designation. In other churches, it has led to ongoing battles. Larger denominations which tend to espouse a more conservative approach include the Southern Baptist Convention and the Lutheran Churches of the Missouri Synod.

Fundamentalist churches are similar to evangelical/conservative churches. The term fundamentalist itself tends to come out of a movement which grew out of concern that fundamental Biblical doctrines were being cast aside by Christian 'modernists.' While there is significant crossover and many who consider themselves fundamentalists would find themselves at home in more conservative churches, Fundamentalism has been a strong force in propelling independent preachers who have broken away from denominational ties. This independence phenomenon is an important ingredient within Protestant Christianity. Many churches have sprung up which are affiliated with other churches but do not foster the strong denominational ties one would find in the mainline churches. Among the conservative churches, fundamentalists tend to be in the forefront of arguments against evolution, climate change and other 'secular' beliefs that run counter to a literal understanding of the Bible. Evangelical/conservative churches might have a broader range on these issues and focus more on matters of personal salvation.

Pentecostalism places less emphasis on actual doctrine and more on the 'experience of the spirit' moving in the heart of the believer. Widespread throughout the frontier and in the south, one sees this approach in such denominations as the Assemblies of God and in congregations/movements led by those who come out of a 'faith healing' tradition. Examples would include Oral Roberts, Rex Humbard and the like.

In recent years, a new Emergent church phenomenon has burst onto the ecclesiastical scene which seeks to integrate a variety of worship practices from the varied Christian traditions and sees itself as post denominational, i.e. these are churches for whom ties to established denominations are of little concern. Emergent Christianity provides flexibility in integrating many traditional spiritual practices with a liberal approach to many issues and with a theology often referred to as "progressive Christianity."

Much of American Protestant Christianity has been shaped by individuals or groups who have broken off from more established Protestant church communities, be they denominations or local congregations. One source indicates that there are more than likely over 40,000 different Protestant denominations in the world! One can say that American notions of freedom and independence have worked cooperatively in shaping the tendencies of American Protestantism.

CAN ONE DEFINE A PROTESTANT?

If a Catholic were to look at this situation within Protestantism which I have described, it might be natural to ask whether it is possible to pin down exactly what it is Protestants share in common, if anything at all! I would contend that, in going back to the roots of the Protestant movement in Middle Ages Europe, one sees a dominant theme:

10

Christian faith transcends human authority. Church laws, rules regulations and practices are all subservient to the role Jesus Christ plays in our own personal salvation and the way we live out our lives. Saying this is a clear defining Protestant tendency does **not mean** a Catholic can't believe it. Instead it strikes me as a direct and accurate way of explaining what was happening in those 16th century battles in Europe which formed the historic basis of Protestantism and which continue to define the heart of the movement today.

LUTHER AND THE PROTESTANT MOVEMENT

Not all Protestants are Lutherans; in fact, most are not. However, one simply cannot understand Protestantism without looking at the life of the Catholic Augustinian priest, Father Martin Luther, and how he evolved into so powerful a figure in the history of the Reformation.

In summary, as Luther grew as a person and faced his own life and his academic work, he discovered that his religious faith was a matter of extreme personal importance. He felt a tension between the way the institutional church was expressing faith in Jesus and what was going on in his heart and soul and in the lives of those he taught and to whom he ministered. He was troubled by the practice of selling and buying indulgences and the notion that one could earn one's salvation through the performance of certain religious works.

While Luther, by his own definition, was a 'loyal son of the church,' he came to understand that faith entailed a personal experience with the Christ who could be found in Scripture! Thus, from Luther's existential experience, came two key tenets of what has come to be known as Protestant Christianity:

» The individual person can see Christ in the Bible. We need to remember that one of Luther's passions was his commitment to getting the Bible in the hands of ordinary people!

11

» The conscience of the individual transcends the law of the institutional church. One who chooses to delve more deeply into Luther will see here is where we locate his powerful teaching that human beings are justified before God by faith.

While future Protestant churches in Europe and eventually in America have looked different from one another and have taken on the influences of those who shaped them (example: Zwingli, Calvin, Wesley, American Calvinist preachers, etc), Luther's affirmations have stood at the heart of Protestantism from the day he was told he could no longer see himself as part of the Catholic Church.

From Luther's affirmations have come the impetus for specific teachings and styles of governance in Protestant churches even when those approaches are different in varied ways from the positions of Luther himself. As a matter of fact, it is important to realize the following:

» Martin Luther was a Catholic.
» He did not set out to start a new church or break away from Catholicism.
» Many of his affirmations, including his writings on justification by faith, have been accepted by later Catholic popes.
» His unwillingness to recant on his opinions led to the Pope's decision to insure his excommunication from Catholicism and provided the impetus for the development of what have come to be known as 'Protestant' churches, known in Luther's terminology not as 'Protestant,' but rather as 'evangelical.'
» In my view, understanding the starting point for the emergence of Protestantism is helpful in exploring how Protestants and Catholics can learn from each other in this,our modern context!

I strongly recommend that Catholics interested in delving more deeply into the life and work of Martin Luther see the film, *Luther*, which was released in 2003 and starred Joseph Fiennes in the title role. It is historically accurate, balanced, and deeply moving!

THE PRACTICAL EFFECT OF THE REFORMATION – OR A GUIDE TO WHAT CATHOLICS WILL FIND IN PROTESTANT CHURCHES

Ultimately, a Roman Catholic seeking to learn about Protestantism for whatever reason will at some point ask the basic questions: What are the differences? What are the different points of emphasis between the Catholic Church and Protestantism? While there is no one simple answer, what you will find below is a guide to what a Catholic will see as he/she explores Protestantism and reads about it and worships in Protestant churches. Contained within these answers are some important emphasis points:

» **A strong emphasis on preaching.** In stating this, one is **not** saying preaching is not important in Roman Catholicism. As a matter of fact, when I was a candidate for diaconal ordination in the Catholic Church, I was the beneficiary of a very strong homiletics (preaching) training program and the influence of my Catholic priest instructor remains with me as I prepare my sermons for my current congregation. Saying this simply affirms the long standing Protestant commitment to this ministry of the Word. In earliest Reformation days, preaching was the important means by which people could be led back into the Bible. In basic terms, the Bible is where one found the activity of God and the revelation about Jesus. In addition, as in many Protestant churches, Communion was celebrated with less frequency than in the Catholic Church, the preeminence of preaching grew significantly. The sermon became the center of the worship service, not part of the ritual which led to the reception of Communion. Many Protestants see worship without Communion as a full experience of worship. Catholics see the reception of Communion as integral to what constitutes public worship.

13

» **Congregational hymn singing.** As Protestantism grew and Protestant worship developed, the active participation of people in the congregation received ever greater prominence. A means of participation that took on enormous popularity was the singing of hymns. The Reformation kicked off an outstanding tradition of hymn writing that has been part of the culture of many Protestant churches. Catholics are often surprised when attending Protestant services by how Protestants tend to sing all the verses of all of the hymns, something one does not always experience in a Catholic church.

» **An emphasis on fellowship.** As an outgrowth of Protestantism's attentiveness to the church as a community of believers sharing in the work of the local congregation, Protestant churches are inclined to see community time or 'fellowship' as part of the Sunday morning routine. While this practice has grown within Catholicism, for many Catholics the central focus of weekend worship has been the act of attending Mass and receiving Communion. While coffee hours have been and are seen as good, they have not been as integral to the Catholic worship experience as they have been for Protestants. One could say that fellowship is part of the "Gestalt" of the Protestant worship experience.

» **The congregation's say in decision making in the church.** One of the dominant themes of the Reformation, the *'priesthood of all believers,'* has influenced how Protestants structure their congregations. As a general rule, local Protestant churches own their buildings and have decision making power regarding who will serve as their pastors. While there are variations between and among denominations, the Protestant congregant expects to have a significant say in important congregational decisions. The Catholic hope and expectation, on the other hand, is that the bishop will send the parish a good pastor who will, in turn, engage the parishioners in the work of leadership in the parish!

» **Little emphasis on following particular rules as stated by a church authority.** In the Roman Catholic Church, there are laws of conduct often determined by Popes and Church Councils. Examples include the prohibition of abortion and contraception, rules for divorce and remarriage, as well as many others. In Protestantism, even the most conservative churches, ones which condemn certain behaviors, tend to focus on that behavior as clearly and unequivocally condemned in the Bible. Catholics speak in terms of Scripture **and** Tradition. This approach acknowledges the specific **teaching authority** of the church, a concept that is not part of the most conservative Protestant approach. More moderate to liberal Protestant churches emphasize the role of the individual human conscience before God. Mixed into this is the long standing popular understanding of Protestantism's notion of 'private interpretation' of Scripture. This notion is based on the assertion that Scripture speaks to each person in the privacy of her/his conscience. There are those within Protestantism who admit to concern with taking this position to its extreme.

» **A strong focus on the Bible.** As indicated in my first point, this 'back to the Bible' emphasis was one of the triggers of the 16th century Reformation itself. It is thus typical, to this day, to find Bibles in the pew racks in Protestant churches and Sunday School curricula based on stories found in Scripture. It should be noted that this characteristic is historic within Protestantism. Since the Second Vatican Council (1962-65), Catholic religious education publishers have produced materials that, in my view, are quite strong in their use of the Bible. It is important to say, however, that much of Catholic religious education is driven by preparation for the celebration of sacraments such as Reconciliation, Communion, and Confirmation. Strong Catholic catechetical programs integrate Biblical teaching closely with this sacramental preparation.

POTENTIAL CATHOLIC PROBLEMS WITH PROTESTANTISM

It is important to point out that as Catholics seek to learn more about Protestantism and as they visit Protestant churches, they may encounter difficulties with some of the practices of Protestant faith. They may wonder why Protestants do things the way they do or, more accurately perhaps, do **not** do certain things that Catholics do. Here are a few areas in which these difficulties might flare up:

1. As I noted above, in many Protestant churches, it is possible to attend a Sunday worship service and not receive Communion. Actually, with the exception of some Protestant denominations (The Episcopal Church, for example), most weekly Protestant worship takes place **without** the celebration of Communion. To be honest, as Protestants and Catholics have come together to study the history of the early church, a good number of Protestants in different traditions have questioned why Protestants celebrate communion as infrequently as they do. Having said this, most Protestant churches see what is known as a Service of the Word as an important and significant act of worship. Those raised Catholic have grown up in a church wherein the normative, ideal worship service is what Catholics call 'The Mass.' In this expression of worship, the culminating event is the consecration of the bread and wine and the subsequent reception of Holy Communion. Ideally, Mass is celebrated daily in local Catholic parishes and in chapels on Catholic college and high school campuses. Daily and weekly Mass are so much a part of Catholic worship practice that many Catholics have a hard time adjusting to its absence in local Protestant congregations, or with the advent of the priest shortage, its absence in their own. This explains why many who leave the Catholic Church have been drawn to churches which tend to retain a 'Catholic feel' e.g. the Episcopal as well as many Lutheran churches. Having said that, there is significant growth in the number of former

Catholics affiliating with churches which have had a 'less Catholic' worship style, including in my own denomination, the United Church of Christ.

2. Churches might seem bare and church experiences pretty basic. To the person raised Catholic who has spent little time inside of Protestant church buildings, many of them, especially those built in the style of a New England meetinghouse, may seem rather bare. Nowhere to be found are statues, Jesus hanging on the Cross, or candles that are lighted all of the time. Gone is the smell of incense to which many Catholics have grown accustomed, as it tends to just remain in a church for quite a while after a funeral! Walk into most Protestant churches and you won't find Stations of the Cross on the walls. You'll rarely see any representation of Mary or any other well known 'saint.' Delve deeper and you would most likely never see anyone praying in front of a tabernacle or clutching rosary beads in her/his hand.

3. In most Protestant churches, you won't see people bending on their knee in the act of genuflection or making the Sign of the Cross gesture on one's body with or without holy water.

4. What is interesting is that, as in the case of the Communion issue, many 'low church' Protestants, i.e. those who have been far removed historically from the 'Catholic' style of worship, have been rethinking their approach. Thus, even in those old meetinghouses, you will now see banners up on the walls and the colors changing with the seasons of the church year, something that was uncommon in many Protestant churches even a generation ago. So, while we **are** seeing an ecumenical convergence wherein Protestants learn from Catholics and vice versa, it remains **fair** to say that there are certain Catholic tendencies whose absence may create barriers for Catholics feeling comfortable in Protestant churches.

5. Many favorite devotions/traditions are missing! In Protestant churches, Catholics won't find certain practices that are part and parcel of their experience with the Catholic faith.

Depending on one's particular Catholic upbringing, the absence of some of the following may seem like a void which exists within the Protestant experience: Benediction of the Blessed Sacrament, Corpus Christi processions, Feast Days for saints, patron saints, the Rosary, Marian crowning, etc, the pageantry of the First Communion celebration! In fact, the absence of any kind of 'devotion' to Mary might be more than many Catholics feel they could handle. It is important to note these devotions and traditions, while part of the Catholic expression of faith for many, may very well be completely absent from the lived experience of many who see themselves as practicing Catholics. One notable exception may very well be the First Communion tradition! Many Catholics who consider Protestantism find themselves troubled when their child receives Communion for the first time in church and tends to be treated without all of the preparation and excitement attached to the Catholic experience of First Communion. Catholics also should be aware of the fact that, in the last two decades, there has been deepened interest in Mary, Jesus' mother, within Protestant preaching and music. The popularity of the modern Christmas classic, *Mary, Did You Know?* is a noteworthy example of this.

6. Oftentimes, there is no clear cut sense of what is right and wrong! Many Catholics who have struggled with what they see as the **legalism** of their church, often around issues of divorce and remarriage, welcome the new found openness they have discovered within many Protestant churches. Yet this same openness has led other Catholics to be uncomfortable. Many Catholics will tell you that even when they disagree with a church's teaching, at least you know where the church stands. In the eyes of many Catholics looking at Protestantism, there is too much uncertainty within it. Protestants, of course, would be inclined to see a certain strength in the fact their tradition emphasizes the primacy of individual conscience, a fact many more 'progressive' Catholics likewise emphasize as congruent

with their tradition. Having said all of this, many Catholics who look at Protestantism find strength in Catholicism's historic tendency to stand very publicly for and against certain behaviors and ways of looking at the world. In short, they see Protestantism as lacking a certain **authority**!

In Protestantism, there is no outward sign of unity. Make no mistake about it.... The Pope is important to Catholics! This does not mean Catholics will necessarily follow the teachings of the church as declared by the Pope. What it does mean is that they tend to take solace in the fact that there is a Pope and he is a figure who is of enormous importance on the world stage.

As this little book is being written, we are in the early stages of the Papacy of Pope Francis I. Those who advocate for the importance of the Papacy will point to the enormous influence this relatively new Pope has already had. Yet, even as Catholics of various persuasions have had differences of opinion with particular Popes and church policies, they tend to be united in the belief that the Papacy has a valuable function within the church and the world and is an important distinguishing mark of the Catholic Church.

While many Catholics fall far short of yearning for a Protestant leader to give authoritative teachings for Christians to follow, they see the presence of the one whom they acknowledge as 'successor to Peter' being of immense value in the church, the absence of which, as is the case with Protestant churches, is noteworthy.

A final note in this area: While it is sad to say, there remain today vestiges of anti-Catholicism within Protestant Christianity. While this is far from being a defining characteristic of Protestantism, it does still exist. While it tends to be found in the more conservative Protestant churches, it exists even in the more moderate or progressive ones. The roots of these different expressions contain their own unique histories. Unfortunately, many Protestant settings are comfortable places to bash Catholic thinking and practices. In my view, to pretend to a Catholic seeking to understand Protestants that there is no longer any anti-Catholicism around is simply dishonest. As a Protestant, I have had to explain and defend Catholicism on numerous occasions. However, to argue that it represents the heart of Protestantism and defines it in any way, would be absolutely irresponsible. Anti-Catholicsm or anti-Protestantism (which clearly exists in some pockets of Catholic practice) impedes the important work of ecumenical Christianity I describe below.

THE ECUMENICAL CENTER

There are many reasons why it is important for Roman Catholics and Protestants to both understand and respect each other. First among them is the simple fact: **both traditions are committed to following Jesus and to the realities of discipleship.** Related to this is another obvious fact: Jesus, as we have said, in a moment of prayer not long before He was killed, pleaded for those who would be His followers might *'all be one.'*

In even more pragmatic terms, Protestants and Catholics live in a world in which they need to interact with each other. In this world, discord and disunity among those who claim to be Christian offers an inadequate witness to those outside of the Christian tradition. It should also be said this it provides a poor example to those within it as well, especially to the young and to individuals who, for whatever reason, feel marginalized in their Christian identity, this disunity often serving as a contributing cause.

For the past several decades, the number of marriages between Protestants and Catholics has been on the increase. In these ecumenical homes, decisions have to be made about the tradition(s) in which the children will be raised. In many situations, one spouse has allowed the children to be raised in the tradition of the other. This has often been the Protestant yielding to the Catholic because of how the traditional Catholic marital promise has been perceived, yet it has often been the husband simply giving in to the religious preference of the children's mother. Unfortunately, many families have missed built-in opportunities to live out their family lives in a true spirit of Christian unity, with the potential for incorporating gifts from each spouse's tradition stifled and allowed to remain dormant.

Yet even as people make their personal choices for a variety of good reasons, it is important to realize the importance of interacting with each other and in sharing Christian faith together, even if they identify with different churches within the larger Christian tradition. Practically speaking, our daughter was married three years ago to a Baptist in a ceremony held in a Roman Catholic chapel. Because of the core of common beliefs we share, it was quite easy, natural and nourishing for me, a Protestant, to share in the profound prayer experience which that marriage ceremony truly was.

In other words, it is my view that there exists an ecumenical center uniting Catholics and Protestants i.e. a core of beliefs and a way of looking at the world. It is this center Catholics and Protestants need to focus on as we interact with each other. The recognition of this center does not downplay or diminish theological differences or each tradition's approach to church governance or worship. Instead it both affirms what we have in common and places those commonalities as having a higher place than the differences on any hierarchy of values the unique traditions may share in common. I will seek to give a specific, concrete example here of exactly what I mean.

As a Protestant I do not accept the idea that having a Mass offered 'for the repose of the soul' for someone who has died can have any effect on how long he/she remains in Purgatory. This, of course, is part of a devotional approach a lifelong Catholic might find missing as she/he explores Protestantism. This notion of praying **for** the dead in order to make an impact upon their eternal status is not part of a common core I might share with a 'traditional' Catholic. However, when I attend a Catholic Funeral Mass, I am united with the Catholic in our shared faith in the Resurrection of Jesus and the effect of that Resurrection upon the eternal life of the one who has died. In other words, faith in the Resurrection is more important than faith in Purgatory!

This faith in the Resurrection of Christ holds a **far** higher place on the hierarchy of values than does a belief in Purgatory or intercession for the deceased. Thus, despite our differences, we, as Protestant and Catholic, can be touched by the same Scripture, sing the same hymns and, for the most part, participate in the prayers of the Mass of the Resurrection, the Catholic funeral liturgy. Saying this is not to make a theological case either for or against the Catholic understanding of Purgatory. It is rather to affirm the ecumenical center around which Christians of different traditions may unite.

Now this matter of a common core has taken on some interesting mutations on the American political scene. The phenomenon of the alliance between fundamentalist Protestants and conservative Catholics through the Moral Majority organization is a good example of this. The 2012 Presidential campaign of conservative Catholic Richard Santorum is an obvious one as well. Senator Santorum's traditional Catholic views on the family and on abortion resonated with many conservative Protestant Christians. Likewise, I have found that for mainline Christians, Protestant and Catholic alike, there are built-in tensions in our attempts to forge ecumenical relations with other Christians, often in our own local communities. Certain hot button issues become litmus tests by which members of other traditions may very well find themselves judged. Two out of many examples come readily to mind:

Several years ago, I was involved in an ecumenical youth ministry project in which we attempted to bring together teenagers from fifteen to twenty local congregations, Protestant and Catholic alike, to enjoy recreation, social time, food (of course!) as well as serious discussion and shared prayer together. In one session which I facilitated involving young Christians from a mainline tradition with a local youth group of more conservative evangelicals, the chasm between the two groups on one particular issue was incredibly deep and very, very wide.

The issue was whether someone who was not Christian (e.g. a Jew) could get to heaven. The mainliners in the group tended toward the position that God made everyone and intends all to be saved. The evangelicals among us held firm to the Biblical injunction that you would only really be saved if you called upon the name of the Lord Jesus. Those more conservative young people expressed their belief that the rest of the group was simply not following Biblical Christianity. Now my view, as one who has worked for a long while in youth ministry, encourages this as great discussion material! Yet, from the perspective of a conservative youth pastor or young person, it's Christians such as I who are really the problem.

In another example, I have found myself in situations where, as a member of a local ecumenical clergy association, the views of the mainline church I represented clashed with other ministerial leaders who exerted leadership positions within the association. In one particular case, a local ministerial leader was responsible for publishing a directory of local clergy, an in house document for those who served in the pastoral role in our churches. This minister also listed the names of our spouses. However, he refused to list the name of a homosexual pastor's partner at a time when Connecticut state law had not yet allowed same sex marriage.

It is my honest belief that even in situations such as these, the quest for shared faith and Christian unity remains essential. It is also extremely difficult because one should never concede on positions considered integral to one's own expression of faith. In an example I gave above, I must say I could never take the stance that a Jew cannot enter God's eternal realm. For me to posit that or to back down on issues of marriage equality would be antithetical to my conscience and to my beliefs. Nonetheless, it is my obligation as a Christian to seek the unity of which Jesus spoke as best as I can, even when my fellow Christians think I belong outside of their circle. Therefore, I must strive to participate, as best as I am able and so far as my conscience will allow, in worthwhile ecumenical ventures in the areas of prayer, service to and advocacy on behalf of others.

The evidence shows, however, that there exists a remarkable common bond of beliefs between most mainline Protestants and Roman Catholics. Large numbers of Catholics do not hold to some of the more traditional church teachings on such matters as divorce and remarriage, legalized abortion, the acceptance of same sex marriage and contraception, to name several controversial items. The great dissent within the Catholic Church over several of these crucial issues has rendered the difference between practicing Catholics and practicing Protestants on these issues negligible at best. Large numbers of Catholic couples are living together and having sex before marriage as are large numbers of their Protestant counterparts. There is no discernible difference in contraception and abortion rates between Catholics and Protestants, nor a significantly reduced number of divorces, despite the official Church teaching on the indissolubility of marriage. When marriages break down, a relatively small number of Roman Catholics proceed with the church's approved procedure in order to procure a declaration of marital nullity. The general comfort level many Catholics feel in receiving Communion in Protestant churches would be of great concern to Catholic traditionalists as are some of the facts concerning adherence to official church teaching which I have just pointed out.

I do not mention any of this to point accusatory fingers at Catholic teaching. I do so instead to indicate there is a strong ecumenical center that currently exists in which great numbers of practicing Catholics and Protestants play a part. Despite different upbringings and traditions, they share much in common:

1. Faith in God and a recognition that God has created human beings and cares for us out of love. While there are different operative theologies within both Catholic and Protestant tradition, between them is a shared faith in the divine activities of creation, redemption and sanctification. In traditional language, this is expressed in such words as Father, Son and Holy Spirit.

2. Belief in Jesus, including faith in the Resurrection and an emphasis on Jesus as the example for human living. This includes an emphasis on the forgiving, loving nature of Jesus'

life. The concept of Jesus as Savior and 'Word Made Flesh' is common language shared by mainline Protestants and Catholics.

3. A sense that the presence of faith does not diminish or excuse the function of human reason. Most recognize that the Bible is an important and central source for revelation, but also God speaks to us through human experience.

4. The complementary belief that scientific knowledge and the use of our minds and religious faith are not incompatible. Most Christians, be they Catholic or Protestant, accept that one can believe Scripture while still accepting the validity of scientific discovery, including the plausibility of accepting both evolution and the existence of God.

5. The importance of prayer and worship. Most Christians affirm the importance of coming together in worship, at least on some occasions.

6. The importance of celebrating and affirming significant life events through ritual. For most Christians, baptizing, sharing Communion, praying for the sick, celebrating marriage and developing rituals for times of loss are important aspects of their communal life of faith. This includes the value of educating young people in these important practices.

7. The value of shared Communion. The issue here is not about how the practices of sharing differ. It is about the concept!

8. The necessity of putting Christian faith in practice through serving others. This includes a strong emphasis on reaching out to those in need.

9. The importance of human relationships and committed love. One could even posit that most see the commitment of marriage as the ideal.

10. The centrality of conscience in making moral decisions.

In more specifically theological terminology and language, one could readily contend that most Protestants and Catholics hold beliefs within shared parameters on the following topics: the presence of grace, the existence of eternal life, the reality of sin, the presence of the Holy Spirit, the centrality of Jesus Christ in revealing divinity, and the sovereignty of God.

SUGGESTIONS FOR INDIVIDUAL CATHOLICS AND LOCAL CHURCHES, BOTH PROTESTANT AND CATHOLIC

These ten indicators constitute an ecumenical center around which mainstream Protestants and Catholics can build. Those on the extreme end of the continuum in both traditions would have serious difficulties with some of these premises. Those who believe a person must belong to the 'one true church' as a necessary condition for salvation would not be comfortable with what I have set forth. In the same way, those who affirm the Bible is inerrant and offers particular prescriptions which exclude certain people from either salvation or membership in the church would have a similar difficulty. In my view, to the fullest extent possible, Christians who hold to this ecumenical center must strive to reach out and walk together with those Christians who differ so strongly with them on these significant matters. I say this acknowledging both the difficulties and the inherent tensions.

Yet, for those Protestants and Catholics who hold to this ecumenical center, there are multiple avenues open for spiritual growth. Within families, in local communities and on a wider scale, committed Catholics and Protestants need to find ways to:

1. Talk to each other about questions of personal faith.
2. Pray together.
3. Study Scripture together.
4. Sing together.
5. Work side by side in mission to those in need.
6. Break down barriers that have stood for a very long time including the barriers around each others' shared rituals as well as barriers surrounding what really constitutes being 'church'.

7. Affirm their disagreements with those both within and outside of their traditions without either being disagreeable or by breaking the bonds of Christian unity.
8. Put the stereotypes and prejudices in the past.
9. Learn more about each others' traditions and explore the incorporation of each others' gifts into their own practice of Christian faith.
10. Seek ways to both discuss and incorporate the notion of what Christian unity really means!

I am hopeful that this little book will help you decide to find ways to make some of these positive actions really happen in your communities!

Closing Words for Catholics from a Protestant Minister Who Loves the Catholic Church

As I sit down to write these words, I do so wondering who will one day read them. I write as someone who has an intense and deep personal regard for the Roman Catholic Church, a regard which has not waned or dissipated in the years since I have become a Protestant. I have written this book for those of you who, like me, have been raised within this Catholic tradition.

In writing this, I am fully aware that our Catholic experiences may have been quite different. I was recently at a Protestant church meeting in which three of the ten people present described themselves as 'recovering Catholics,' the same phrase I heard before at a meeting in a different church just a week prior. I understand that for many people, your experience in the Catholic Church has been a difficult one.

Yet, while I understand that, I have to honestly say that for me, it was a wonderful, life shaping series of experiences and even as I came to the conclusion as a middle aged adult that the best description for myself was as a Protestant, I bring to that Protestantism everything I gained from the incredible intellectual, educational, social justice oriented and spiritual tradition that is Roman Catholicism, even with all of its flaws.

So as you, a Catholic, explore Protestantism for whatever reason, I hope you are able to affirm the strengths of the Catholic tradition, even as you discover what may be for you the new insights that have come from the Protestant experience.

My prayer for you is that the end result will be an appreciation of the richness and the depth that resides even within our incomplete and very human attempt to follow Jesus. He urged all of us, wherever we may have come from or may still go, to do everything in our power to insure that we somehow remain 'One.'

SUGGESTED READING

Brown, Robert McAfee. *The Spirit of Protestantism.* New York: Oxford Press, 1965. (This provides a complete, comprehensive, easy to read overview of both the history of Protestantism and its varieties.)

Kung, Hans. *On Being a Christian.* New York: Doubleday, 1976. (In this work, Dr. Kung explains the strengths of Catholic and Protestant traditions.)

LaRochelle, Robert. *Crossing the Street.* Gonzalez, Florida: Energion, 2012. (This book details my personal journey from Catholicism to Protestantism and offers insights about the strengths of both traditions.)

Lull, Timothy, ed. *Martin Luther's Basic Theological Writings.* Minneapolis: Augsburg Fortress, 1995. (In my view, the best available resource of getting a real taste of what Luther thought and taught, in his own words, with helpful guidance.)

Prothero, Stephen. *Religious Literacy.* San Francisco: Harper San Francisco, 2007. (In my view, this work is a modern religious classic. Dr. Prothero makes a strong case for the practical importance of knowledge of religious history and belief.)

MORE FROM ENERGION PUBLICATIONS

Personal Study
Finding My Way in Christianity	Herold Weiss	$16.99
The Jesus Paradigm	David Alan Black	$17.99
When People Speak for God	Henry Neufeld	$17.99

Christian Living
Faith in the Public Square	Robert D. Cornwall	$16.99
Grief: Finding the Candle of Light	Jody Neufeld	$8.99
Crossing the Street	Robert LaRochelle	$16.99

Bible Study
Learning and Living Scripture	Lentz/Neufeld	$12.99
From Inspiration to Understanding	Edward W. H. Vick	$24.99
Luke: A Participatory Study Guide	Geoffrey Lentz	$8.99
Philippians: A Participatory Study Guide	Bruce Epperly	$9.99
Ephesians: A Participatory Study Guide	Robert D. Cornwall	$9.99
Evidence for the Bible	Elgin Hushbeck, Jr.	

Theology
Creation in Scripture	Herold Weiss	$12.99
Creation: the Christian Doctrine	Edward W. H. Vick	$12.99
Ultimate Allegiance	Robert D. Cornwall	$9.99
History and Christian Faith	Edward W. H. Vick	$9.99
The Church Under the Cross	William Powell Tuck	$11.99
The Journey to the Undiscovered Country	William Powell Tuck	$9.99
Eschatology: A Participatory Study Guide	Edward W. H. Vick	$9.99
Philosophy for Believers	Edward W. H. Vick	$14.99
Christianity and Secularism	Elgin Hushbeck, Jr.	$16.99

Ministry
Clergy Table Talk	Kent Ira Groff	$9.99
So Much Older Then …	Robert LaRochelle	$9.99

Generous Quantity Discounts Available
Dealer Inquiries Welcome
Energion Publications — P.O. Box 841
Gonzalez, FL 32560
Website: http://energionpubs.com
Phone: (850) 525-3916

TOPICAL LINE DRIVES

Straight to the Point in under 44 Pages

All Topical Line Drives volumes are priced at $4.99 print and 99¢ in all ebook formats.

Available

The Authorship of Hebrews: The Case for Paul	David Alan Black
What Protestants Need to Know about Roman Catholics	Robert LaRochelle
What Roman Catholics Need to Know about Protestants	Robert LaRochelle
Forgiveness: Finding Freedom from Your Past	Harvey Brown, Jr.
Process Theology: Embracing Adventure with God	Bruce Epperly

Holistic Spirituality: Life Transforming Wisdom from the Letter of James
Bruce Epperly

To Date or Not to Date: What the Bible Says about Pre-Marital Relationships
D. Kevin Brown

Forthcoming

God the Creator: The Variety of Christian Views on Origins   Henry Neufeld

The Authority of Scripture in a Postmodern Age: Some Help from Karl Barth
Robert D. Cornwall

The Eucharist: Encounters with Jesus at the Table   Robert D. Cornwall

Planned

Render to Caesar	Chris Surber
The Caregiver's Beattitudes	Robert Martin
The Problem with Social Justice	Elgin Hushbeck, Jr.
A Cup of Cold Water	Chris Surber
Christian Existentialism	David Moffett-Moore
Paths to Prayer	David Moffett-Moore

(The titles of planned volumes may change before release.)

Generous Quantity Discounts Available
Dealer Inquiries Welcome
Energion Publications — P.O. Box 841
Gonzalez, FL 32560
Website: http://energionpubs.com
Phone: (850) 525-3916

USE THIS BOOK WITH ITS COMPANION VOLUME
FOR ECUMENICAL STUDY GROUPS

... and in confirmation classes, high school and college campus
ministry and youth ministry settings in your local community

What Protestants Need to Know About Roman Catholics

Robert LaRochelle

Topical
Line
Drives

Volume 2

ALSO FROM ENERGION PUBLICATIONS

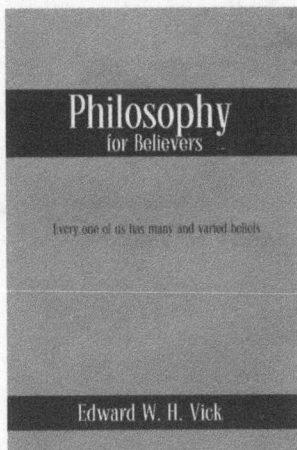

Philosophy
for Believers

Every one of us has many and varied beliefs

Edward W. H. Vick

This work is a marvelous corrective to those who see faith as antithetical to human reason.

Rev. Dr. Robert R. LaRochelle,
Pastor, Second Congregational
Church, Manchester, CT

ALSO BY BOB LAROCHELLE

I highly recommend this book to those who are interested in learning from one man's courageous and joyful journey.

The Rev. Albert R. Cutié
Priest-in-Charge
Church of the Resurrection
Biscayne Park, FL

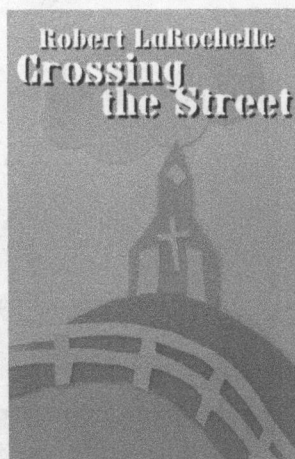

Robert LaRochelle
Crossing
the Street

www.ingramcontent.com/pod-product-compliance
Lightning Source LLC
Chambersburg PA
CBHW011750020426
42331CB00014B/3349

* 9 7 8 1 6 3 1 9 9 0 0 6 9 *